YORK MINSTER

ANN WILLEY

First published in 1998 by Scala Books
143-149 Great Portland Street
London W1N 5FB

Distributed in the USA and Canada by
Antique Collectors' Club
Market Street Industrial Park
Wappingers' Falls
NY 12590
USA

ISBN 1 85759 188 7

Text by Ann Willey
Photographs by
Jim Kershaw: front cover, back cover
and pages 1, 5, 7, 10, 12, 13, 14, 19, 20,
22, 23, 28, 29, 30, 32, 33, 34, 38, 39, 41,
46, 47, 50, 51, 54, 57, 58, 59, 61, 64, 73,
74, 76, 77, 81, 86, 87, 88, 89, 90, 91, 92
Alan Curtis: pages 3, 4, 11, 26, 31, 34, 36, 43,
44, 45, 49, 52, 53, 55, 56, 63, 66, 69, 70, 79
Peter Smith: pages 16, 17
Designed by John Anastasio
Edited by Tim Ayers
Printed and bound in Italy by Grafiche Milani

Front cover image
View of the South Transept
Back cover image
The Minster at night
Title page image
Looking up into the central tower
Opposite
The chapter house vault

CONTENTS

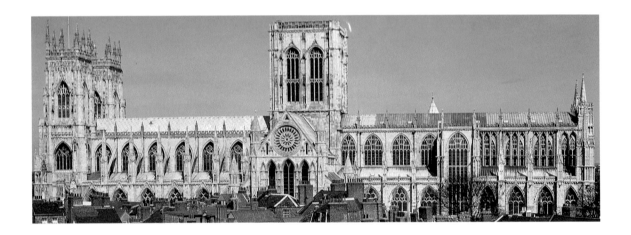

MESSAGE FROM THE ARCHBISHOP

As the largest cathedral church in northern Europe, the Minster dominates the skyline for many miles around the city of York.

Its ancient stones, as warm and mellow in the thin sunlight of a chilly winter as in high summer, tell a story that stretches back to the very roots of Christian England. For York Minster does more than dominate the skyline, it towers over the whole history of Christianity in the north of England. More even than that – as when, for example, Alcuin responded to Charlemagne's call to bring Christian learning to France – it has reached out to shape events across Europe.

But this place represents far more than just another feat of architectural heroism or a grand counterpoint in stone to the chronicle of a nation's history. It was – and is – a living place, a place of pilgrimage, a place of prayer and worship. A place where men and women, commoners and kings, citizens of this country and of countries the world over, have gathered to acknowledge Jesus as their Lord.

I hope you will gain much from your time in York Minster – and I am sure that this excellent book will help you to do exactly that. You will see the beauty and sense the history: but above all, your hearts and minds will be opened to God's greatness and God's glory.

David Ebor

Above. The Minster rises above York's rooftops to dominate the skyline.

Opposite. The east end, showing the Perpendicular style of the east window

CHRONOLOGY

306	Constantine proclaimed Emperor at York
314	Eborius attends Council of Arles
627	Baptism of King Edwin
c. 640	Completion of Oswald's stone church around Edwin's baptistry
766–781	Alcuin, master of cathedral school
972	Oswald appointed Archbishop of York
1070	Thomas of Bayeux appointed Archbishop of York
1075	Last Viking raid on York. Minster badly damaged
c. 1080–1100	New Minster built on present site
1137	East end of Minster damaged by fire
1141	William Fitzherbert elected as Archbishop of York
1143	Consecration of William Fitzherbert
1147	Archbishop William deposed in favour of Henry Murdac
1153	Death of Henry Murdac. Restoration of William as Archbishop of York
1154	Death of William. Roger Pont l'Evêque appointed Archbishop of York
c. 1175	Completion of new choir and crypt
1215	Walter Gray appointed Archbishop of York
c. 1220–1244	Rebuilding of the south transept
1227	Canonization of William Fitzherbert
1251	Marriage of Alexander III of Scotland and Margaret, daughter of Henry III, in the Minster
1253	Rebuilding of the north transept completed
c. 1260	Five Sisters Window completed. Work begun on the chapter house
1284	Translation of St William's remains to the new shrine
1291	Archbishop Romeyn laid the foundation stone for the new nave
1338	Great west window completed
1361	Building of present Lady Chapel begun
c. 1394–1420	Building of present choir
1405–1408	Glazing of the great east window
1407	Partial collapse of the central tower
c. 1420–1465	Rebuilding of the central tower
1472	Re-dedication of the cathedral
1474	Completion of western towers
1650–1660	No Archbishop, Dean or Chapter

1660	Restoration of cathedral clergy and services
1731–1738	Re-paving of the Minster
1829	Choir roof, stalls and organ destroyed by fire
1832	Repairs to east end completed
1840	Nave roof destroyed by fire. Nave and south-west tower badly damaged
1844	Nave repairs completed. New peal of bells
1845	Great Peter installed in north-west tower
1967–1972	Major restoration work to the foundations and central tower
1984	South transept gutted by fire
1988	South transept repairs completed. Queen attends service of re-dedication
1990	The great west window re-dedicated after replacement of the stonework
1993	Choir floor re-paved
1997–1998	Stonework around west door replaced

The Minster from the south-east.

CHAPTER ONE

THE BEGINNINGS

Few people affect significantly the world in which they live. One such person was Constantine the Great who, in 312 CE, first allowed Christianity to become one of the permitted religions of the Roman Empire. In the year 306 CE, he had been in York, standing on the same ground that the Minster now occupies, which was then the site of the Roman fort.

York, or Eboracum, possibly meaning 'the place of the yew trees', had first been established in c. 72 CE, when the Romans made another determined effort to extend their rule over the whole of Britain. The fort they built became the headquarters of the Ninth Legion and the base from which they hoped to suppress the northern tribes. A *colonia* providing civilian housing developed on the south bank of the River Ouse and the two sites made up Eboracum, one of the most important towns in Roman Britain.

Constantine was visiting these military headquarters with his father, Constantius Chlorus, when the latter died. The troops based in Eboracum immediately hailed him as the next Emperor of the West. There were other contenders for the title, but Constantine defeated them, being finally acknowledged as undisputed Emperor in 312 CE. The initial recognition of Constantine's future role was probably made in the *basilica*, or great hall, of the headquarters building, or *principia*, which was sited where the central tower of the Minster now stands.

Tradition states that Constantine was converted to Christianity on the eve of the Battle of Milvian Bridge, the final conflict in his struggle for power. In a vision, he was told that if his soldiers scratched a cross on their shields, then he would win. He ordered them to do this, and was duly victorious. How could he continue to persecute Christians? As

A detail from St Luke's Gospel in the York Gospel Book. Each new canon still takes the Chapter Oath upon it.

he himself was not baptized until he lay dying in 337, there is some doubt about the relative strength of his political and spiritual motives. Nevertheless, his action allowed Christianity to come into the open and begin to gather strength.

There is evidence to suggest that there were Christians already in York at this time, for in 314 a bishop from the city was one of three British bishops to travel to Gaul for the Council of Arles. No archaeological evidence of the building in which they worshipped has so far been found but some artefacts have come to light, including a tile on which has been scratched the chi-rho sign. (This symbol uses the Greek letters chi and rho, which resemble X and P in English but translate as Ch and R, the first letters of the title Christ.)

By the beginning of the 5th century, the Roman forces had been withdrawn from Britain, in an attempt to consolidate and defend the heart of the Empire. This left Britain undefended and open to attack by the Picts and the Saxons, and to their eventual take-over. Any vestige of Christianity disappeared from York as the pagan invaders established the kingdom of Deira. One pocket of Christianity only remained in the area, the small kingdom of Elmet south-west of York, but this too eventually fell to Edwin.

It was Edwin, however, who brought Christianity back to the region, following his own conversion. His wife, Ethelburga, a Christian princess from Kent, did as her own mother, Bertha, had done before her when she persuaded her husband to turn from his pagan gods. Not only he, but also his extended family and court were baptized by Paulinus, the priest sent by Ethelburga's brother, in accordance with the marriage agreement, to accompany her north. The small wooden church built for this ceremony is regarded as York's first Minster.

Again, no archaeological evidence of this building has been found, but Bede, 'the father of English history', gives an

Evidence of Roman occupation - a lion's head, probably part of a harness, found during excavations under York Minster.

account of the events surrounding Edwin's conversion and baptism in his *History of the English Church and People*. He describes the discussion between the king and his counsellors which led to the decision to adopt the new religion. The decision made, a church was needed so that baptisms could take place. Whilst Edwin and his court received instruction in the new faith, builders erected a small wooden baptistry to be ready for use on Easter Day 627. Once the baptisms had been

Early 4th-century head of the Emperor Constantine, from a statue that was twice life-size. The original is in the Yorkshire Museum.

St Peter, patron saint of the Minster, as portrayed in the glass of the north transept.

Right. This elaborate font
cover was designed by Sir
Ninian Comper in 1947 and
depicts those associated
with York's first Minster.
The figures are, from the
left, Queen Ethelburga, King
Edwin, Bishop Paulinus, St
Hilda and James the Deacon.

Above. Part of a Saxon
gravestone found during the
1967–72 excavations under
York Minster.

performed, there was time to begin a larger building project
and Edwin ordered that a stone church should be erected
around the wooden chapel. His death in 632, killed in a
battle with Penda, the pagan King of Mercia, temporarily
halted this work. Paulinus took Ethelburga and her children
back to Kent. Although he never received the pallium, the
symbol of an archbishop's authority given by the Pope,
Paulinus is regarded as the first Archbishop of York. It was
more than 30 years before York again had a bishop, even
though Oswald, having regained the territory lost to Penda,
completed the stone church begun by Edwin. He continued
the tradition of dedicating the church to St Peter, the
dedication which has continued until the present day.

The year 664 saw not only the Synod of Whitby and, with
it, the acceptance of the Roman tradition rather than the
Celtic for the Church in England, but also the appointment of
York's next bishop. Wilfrid. Despite being born in
Northumbria and educated at Lindisfarne, he came from the
Roman tradition. It was not until 669, however, that York was
able to benefit from his efficiency and experience, as he
stayed away five years when he travelled to France for his
consecration. Indeed, despairing of his return, the king had

appointed Chad as bishop in his place. The latter, a gentle man trained by St Aidan in the Celtic tradition, stood down on Wilfrid's reappearance. Wilfrid remained as York's bishop until 691, when the last of several quarrels with the king gave grounds for his expulsion. Whilst bishop, he had repaired the church, leading the roof and glazing the windows for the first time, as well as whitewashing the internal walls.

Bosa, who had already spent some years as Bishop of York during Wilfrid's earlier fall from favour, again returned to the see. In 685, Theodore, the Greek Archbishop of Canterbury, visited York and consecrated St Cuthbert Bishop of Lindisfarne in the Saxon Minster. This was the age when saints and scholars flourished in the North. Another such was York's next bishop, St John of Beverley, who had himself been a pupil of Theodore at the famous school in Canterbury. He was vigorous and active, constantly dedicating new churches, teaching his people and using the Greek medical knowledge learned at Canterbury to heal the sick.

It was not until Ecgbert was consecrated in 732 that the papal pallium reached York and the see became an archbishopric. Ecgbert was the last of York's prelates to have known Bede. The latter advised him as to appropriate behaviour for an archbishop – he should study, particularly St Paul's pastoral letters, teach and train his clergy but, above all, run a household which was given to serious and godly pursuits. Telling stories and jokes should be avoided, as should laughter. Ecgbert was also the first of York's archbishops to influence Alcuin, another famous scholar of the period, and because of this he is often regarded as the founder of the cathedral school. In reality, education had been part of cathedral life since the time of Wilfrid, but Ecgbert expanded and developed both the school and library. Most significantly, he appointed as master Aethelbert, the man who would succeed him as Archbishop. Under Aethelbert's leadership, the school grew and flourished, gaining a reputation far beyond northern England. When, in 782, Charlemagne invited Alcuin to become the master of his own palace school, he was acknowledging York's reputation as a centre of learning.

A carved gravestone from the Saxon cemetery found under the Minster.

Opposite. The beginning of
St Matthew's Gospel in the
York Gospel Book. Made in
Canterbury in c. 1000, it was
brought to York in 1020. It
is one of only ten pre-
Conquest Gospel Books to
have survived the
Reformation.

It was during Ecgbert's tenure of the see, in 741, that the first stone church burned down. There is no evidence to suggest that this was the result of anything but an accident, and that church was then replaced by a much larger and finer building. Once again, with no archaeological evidence on which to base a reconstruction, it is the written word which provides such detail as we have. Alcuin describes the church as lofty, the panelled ceiling being supported by columns with rounded arches between. It contained 30 altars, many of which were housed in side chapels.

It was over a hundred years before the Vikings captured York and there is little detailed knowledge of the period in between. Their trading brought prosperity to the city, and by the 10th century some Danes were converting to Christianity. The Minster remained the centre for Christian worship, but its school and library disappeared. Two Archbishops from this period are worthy of note, Sts Oswald and Wulfstan. Both held the see of Worcester simultaneously with that of York, the justification for this being the paganism of the city and the cathedral's consequent poverty. Certainly both seem to have preferred their southern and more settled diocese, which had at its heart a monastery. The Minster has never been a monastic foundation, for although the name derives from the same source as the word monastery, it originally referred to any church which was a mission-station served by a group of secular clergy living communally.

Below. The Horn of Ulf. This
drinking vessel, made from
an elephant's tusk, was
given to the Minster by a
Viking thane in token of a
gift of land.

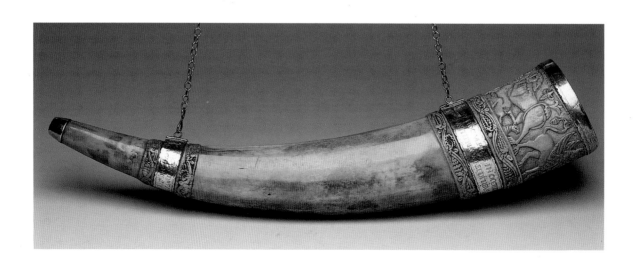

INITIVM EVANGE
LII DNI NRI IHV
XPI SCDM MATHM

LIBER

GENERATIONIS IHV
XPI FILI DAVID·
FILII ABRA
HAM·

ABRAHAM AVTE GENIT ISAAC·
ISAAC AVTEM GENVIT IACOB IACOB AVTE
GENVIT IVDAM ET FRS EIVS IVDAS AV
TEM· GENVIT PHARES ET ZARA DETHA
MAR· PHARES AVTEM· GENVIT

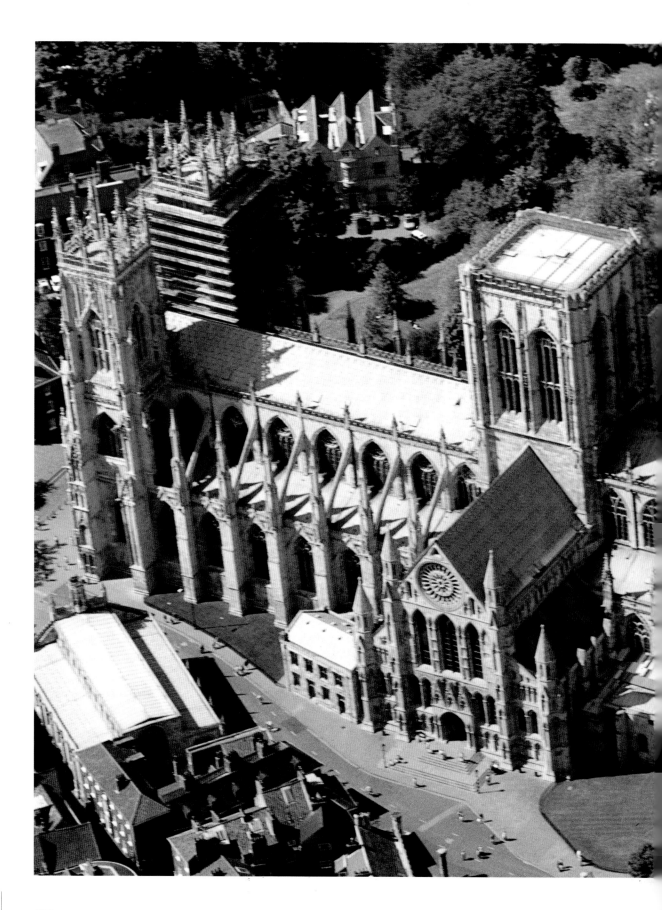

Aerial view of the Minster.

CHAPTER TWO

THE NORMAN MINSTER

The cathedral suffered much greater devastation than that inflicted by the Vikings following the Norman invasion in 1066. The north of England resisted William's attempts to acquire the English throne and paid for this with the 'Harrying of the North', during which all was laid waste. Nor did they succeed in preventing William becoming king. Recognizing the danger of continued rebellion, William strengthened his hold on the throne by giving all positions of authority, influence and importance to fellow-Normans. In this process, York acquired a new Archbishop.

Thomas (1070–1100), who had been Treasurer at Bayeux Cathedral before coming to York, belonged to a priestly family; his brother, Samson, became Bishop of Worcester in 1096 and his nephew, who was also called Thomas, came to York as Archbishop in 1108. These were men with good administrative skills, Samson being identified as the author and chief scribe of the Domesday Book, and Thomas establishing a system of government by which the cathedral has continued to run, its form only slightly modified, until today.

The building which greeted Thomas's eyes on his arrival in York was a sorry sight, burned and pillaged as it had been by the Norman soldiers. Undaunted, he patched up the church, rebuilt the refectory and dormitory, and gathered together some of the scattered clergy so that the daily office could continue. A final blow came in 1075 when the Danes made a last attempt to establish their rule in northern England. Two hundred ships sailed up the Ouse, landing an army of sufficient strength to inflict severe damage on the city. In the course of the fighting, the Minster was badly damaged once more.

Once the Danes had been defeated, Archbishop Thomas decided that, rather than repair the Saxon church again, it was time to choose a new site on which to build a new cathedral. He recognized that the Romans had picked the best ground in the city for the *principia* of their fortress and decided that, as this was now little more than a heap of rubble, that would be the place to build. Archaeologists have excavated under most of the Minster and in doing so have revealed the foundations of his cathedral, so its size and shape are known. As it was 110 metres long, we can surmise that it was much larger than previous cathedrals in York. The shape reflected Thomas's

Norman piers, built to raise Archbishop Roger's Choir, which can still be seen in the western crypt.

The eastern crypt, showing
the re-used Romanesque
capitals.

French background, three semi-circular apses being incorporated into the design of the eastern arm. The nave was large but aisleless.

York is not an ideal site for heavy buildings, for the bedrock is deep below the surface, far deeper than any builder would consider necessary for foundations. To overcome this problem the Norman builders created a raft of huge hewn timbers, laying them across each other and filling the spaces with mortar and rubble. For the walls themselves, which were 2.1 metres thick, they re-used much of the stone from the *principia*. Once the building was complete, they faced it with white plaster on which they painted red lines to indicate the stones' edges. The huge white edifice must have been visible from miles around, towering above all other buildings in the city – and it had taken only 20 years to build.

Archbishop Thomas died in 1100, leaving as his legacy to York a new cathedral with an efficient system of government, but without challenging Canterbury's assumption of primacy in England. Indeed, he had been forced to profess obedience to Archbishop Lanfranc at Canterbury. It was Archbishop Thurstan of York (1114–1140) who first tackled this thorny problem. When Pope Gregory had sent missionaries to England, he dictated that there should be two metropolitan sees (seats of archbishops), one in London and the other in York, and that each should take it in turn to assume seniority. This reflected the importance of both cities during the Roman occupation. St Augustine, however, made Canterbury his headquarters and the southern province centred on that city. As it had been in existence longer and was closer to London, Canterbury had asserted its primacy with some success, York being viewed as a northern outpost.

The case was taken to Rome for adjudication and Hugh the Chanter has left an account of the struggle. He tells how the Canterbury monks used forged documents to prove their case, becoming the laughing-stock of the court when they tried to explain the absence of the seals that would have proved them valid. The Pope could do no other than find in York's favour and since then no Archbishop of York has professed obedience to his counter-part in Canterbury. Thurstan also faced problems

Detail from the portal to the north-east crypt of the rebuilt Norman cathedral.

of a more practical nature, when the east end of the Minster was badly damaged by fire in 1137. Repairs were probably begun during his primacy, but they were not completed until after his death.

Meanwhile, his successor had more pressing worries. William Fitzherbert came from a landed Yorkshire family with royal connections. His mother was the half-sister of King Stephen and his father had been Chamberlain to Henry I, so it was no surprise when William was appointed to the lucrative position of Treasurer of York Minster. When he was elected Archbishop of York, in 1141, the choice was not unanimously popular, however. Indeed, some of the canons, supported by the religious orders which by this time were numerous in the diocese, refused to accept the election, demanding that the Pope should intervene. As they had gained the support of Bernard of Clairvaux, who had great influence with Pope Eugenius III, they succeeded in having William deposed, Henry Murdac being appointed in his stead.

William accepted his fate and went first to Sicily for a year and then to live in the monastery at Winchester where his uncle was bishop. Whilst never taking religious vows, he did change his life-style from one of good-living to an asceticism based on prayer and study. His supporters, for he was very popular in York, did not accept the situation so meekly, however. They burned and pillaged Fountains Abbey and forced the new Archbishop to flee from York to Beverley.

In 1153, William's fortunes changed once again, for in that year, Henry Murdac, the Pope and St Bernard all died, and he was restored to York much to the delight of the citizens. He was making a triumphant entry into the city when he reached the bridge over the River Ouse. Far too many people had crowded on to it, causing the structure to collapse under their combined weight! Seeing this disaster, William stopped and

A scene from a Doom stone, showing those condemned to Hell, originally part of an external frieze on the Norman cathedral. This can now be seen in the crypt.

Archbishop William Fitzherbert, as portrayed in the Bolton Book of Hours.

· S· Wilims·

called on God to save all from drowning. No lives were lost.

Within a few months of his return to the city, William was dead, believed poisoned. He had been taken ill after celebrating early Mass and Osbert, Archdeacon of Richmond, stood accused of adding poison to the chalice. The latter, unable to prove his innocence, was unfrocked and became a minor baron. Stories of miraculous healings began to be associated with the site of William's burial and when, in 1223, a sweet-smelling oil seeped from his tomb, people became convinced that he was a saint. In 1227 the Archbishop was officially canonized and his body moved to a shrine behind the High Altar – but this is to move too quickly through York's story.

William's successor, Roger Pont l'Evêque, the candidate of King Stephen, the Archbishop of Canterbury and the suspect Archdeacon of Richmond was elected with such haste that even contemporaries commented. A worldly, ambitious prelate, Roger was happy to support Henry II in his struggle to gain control in the Church. This brought both men into conflict with the newly appointed Archbishop of Canterbury, Thomas Becket, and led eventually to Becket's murder – an event for which Roger was blamed by many.

Roger's greatest achievement was to rebuild the damaged eastern arm of the Minster. He remodelled the choir, raising it on enormous weight-bearing Norman pillars, the remains of which can still be viewed in the crypt. He squared off the apses built under Thomas's instruction, adding small transepts and an ambulatory to improve circulation during services. Some of the glass made for the windows of this new east end survives

to this day, reused in the upper windows of the nave. The
main transepts were extended at this time, making them the
length they are today. He remodelled the west end also,
adding towers and a chapel close to the north-west corner of
the nave. By 1181, when Roger died, York had been turned
into one of the great cathedrals of Europe and by the early
13th century its fame had spread beyond the Alps.

Geoffrey Plantagenet, the illegitimate son of Henry II,
was chosen to succeed Roger and he was an even more
political animal than his predecessor. As he had also inherited
his father's temper, he spent most of his reign quarrelling with

the Chapter in York and his brothers, Richard the Lionheart and King John. When Richard was captured by the Saracens whilst on crusade, Geoffrey rallied to his cause, however, and sent the cathedral's treasure as part of the ransom. The Chapter eventually bought it back. He, himself, ended his days in France in exile, dying in 1212.

Although the Chapter objected initially to the appointment of Walter Gray to the see after Geoffrey's death, his 40-year rule marked a period during which York prospered. This was the time when the cathedral we know today began to be built.

Panels of 12th-century Romanesque glass now to be found in the windows of the clerestory.

CHAPTER THREE

RE-BUILDING THE TRANSEPTS

The election of a successor to Geoffrey took time and eventually required the intervention of the Pope, Innocent III. Walter Gray was seen initially as a royal appointee, as he had been the Chancellor of England, supporting King John at Runnymede when he put his seal to Magna Carta. Accused by the York Chapter of being illiterate, Gray was eventually if reluctantly, accepted. From 1215 to his death in May 1255, Walter worked to reform the administration of the province and tightened that of the Minster, defining, for example, the terms of residence for clergy appointed as residentiary canons.

He is best remembered, however, for the building work that he instigated. French cathedrals and even Canterbury had begun to build in the new Gothic style. The pointed arches allowed buildings to soar upwards to a greater height than their Romanesque counterparts, an important image at a time when heaven was believed to be above the earth. Walter persuaded the Dean and Chapter that the Minster should be rebuilt in this style and he did much to help fund the work. The south transept was completed in his lifetime, phase one of a building project which would take roughly 250 years to complete.

Funding such a huge undertaking also required organization and Walter set about this task, also collecting alms and granting indulgences to those who contributed. He persuaded the great local landowners to support the work. Robert Vavasour granted rights to quarry stone at Tadcaster, and to pass over his land in order to obtain stone from Thevesdale. The Percy family contributed oaks with which to construct the huge vault of the roof. It had been recognized that the building would be too huge to support the weight of traditional stone vaulting.

Later archbishops used other money-raising devices. Much of the heraldry which can be seen in the stone and glass of the Minster was the result of their efforts during the re-building of the nave, when a gift towards the fabric was rewarded by the inclusion of the family's arms.

The south transept. The first
part of the present building
to be completed. None of the
glass is contemporary with
the stonework.

Left. The altar in St Michael's Chapel. The design for the embroidered altar frontal was based on one of the medieval Resurrection symbols found on the cushion in Walter Gray's tomb during restoration work in 1968.

Without doubt, one of the sources of greatest financial help came with the establishment of the shrine of St William, who had been canonized in 1227. No longer did pilgrims by-pass York on their way to the shrines at Beverley or Ripon. The Minster now became a focus for their journeys and gifts. In 1284 Edward I helped to carry the coffin when it was taken from the site of William's original interment in the nave to the newly erected shrine behind the High Altar. His head, however, did not make this journey, for, placed in a silver-gilt reliquary studded with jewels, this was kept apart and became one of York's most famous treasures.

One of only three royal weddings to be celebrated in the Minster occurred during the archbishopric of Walter Gray. In 1251, Henry III's daughter, Margaret, married Alexander III of Scotland. Hosting the wedding cost Walter four thousand marks, as he not only donated 60 oxen for the feast but also provided lodgings for those with nowhere to stay and pasture for the horses.

Walter was buried in the newly finished south transept of the Minster, where he had ordained his chantry at the altar of St Michael. There is a boss depicting Michael in the vaulting above and later, in the 15th century, the window behind was decorated with the figure of the archangel. Originally the canopy over his tomb was coloured, and the whole monument is a superb

Below. The Purbeck marble effigy of Archbishop Walter Gray.

Looking towards the north transept, where the crib is placed at Christmas and a Children's service is held on Christmas Eve.

The rose, or more properly, the wheel window at the apex of the south transept gable.

example of 13th-century art. Restoration earlier this century revealed that the lid of the coffin had been decorated with a painting of the Archbishop in full canonicals, and buried with him had been his archiepiscopal ring, pectoral cross and crosier, as well as a chalice and paten. These artefacts can now be seen amongst the exhibits in the Treasury.

Of far greater beauty than the south transept is its equivalent to the north. This is associated particularly with John Romanus and was begun whilst he was Treasurer. Whereas the main south transept wall is broken by two tiers of doubled lancet windows under a rose, that on the north is filled with the simple beauty of the Five Sisters Window – five tall lancets in Early English style. These contain the largest amount of grisaille glass found in a single composition anywhere in the world. Since 1260, much of the glass has been replaced by restoration insertions and the ancient glass that survives has suffered corrosion and paint loss, so that the appearance of the window has changed dramatically and permanently from its original state.

The window was last restored in 1924, having been removed for safety during the First World War. Re-leading was necessary before it could be replaced, but, although the lead had been given by the Trust which managed the Earl of Feversham's

The north transept, showing the Five Sisters Window.

estate, following a discovery of ingots during excavations at Rievaulx Abbey, the Dean and Chapter could not afford to pay for the work. The money was raised eventually by a York woman, following a vision she experienced one evening in the Minster. In this, she saw her two younger sisters, who had been dead for many years, beckoning her towards the empty window. As they faded from her sight, they were replaced by five women, sitting in a garden, sewing. Inspired by the idea that the window could become a memorial to the women of the British Empire who had been killed in the War, she launched an appeal and the money needed for the work was quickly raised.

On Midsummer Day 1925, the Queen Mother, then the Duchess of York, unveiled the restored window. Nearby, painted on oak screens are the names of fourteen hundred women killed in the fighting of the First World War, the most famous being Nurse Edith Cavell. The window is now also a memorial to the even greater number of women killed during the Second World War.

The wooden vaulting of the north transept. The Percy family, which donated the wood during the building of the present Minster, is commemorated in the design by its coat of arms, a blue lion on a gold background.

No other medieval Archbishop was to hold the see for as long as Walter Gray. The seven prelates who followed him were in the main promoted from the Chapter of York and, in consequence, their interests lay in the city and its Minster, which was fortunate as the building work was still on-going.

During the 14th century, the services of the Minster were conducted in what must have seemed more like a building site than a house of prayer. The slow development of the Gothic cathedral brought changes to the furnishings inside, as did the growing liturgical complexity of worship during this period. Chantry altars increased steadily, until the Reformation put an end to the practice of saying masses for the souls of the dead. It is believed that by the middle of the 15th century there were 60 such altars in the building, necessitating special housing for the priests who serviced them. This was St William's College, built at the eastern end of the cathedral precincts, which today is used as the Minster's education and conference centre.

Above. A selection of bosses from the vaulting of the north transept.

Not all the purposes for which the cathedral was used at this time were religious. Rents were paid inside the Minster – sometimes on the High Altar itself! The cathedral was thought to be a place of safe-keeping by local merchants, including Jews, who deposited their valuables into its care. It was, inevitably, used for convocations and synods of the Northern Province, but, it was also used by the city council for its meetings. In the early 1330s the chapter house was used as the royal chancery. The rebuilding of this had been completed 50 years previously, specifically to accommodate the secular aspects of cathedral life.

Detail from the brass memorial to Archbishop William Greenfield (1306–1315). This is the only surviving medieval brass in the Minster and the earliest surviving episcopal brass in England.

The Hindley clock on the east wall of the north transept. Its movement was made in 1749 by the York clockmaker, Henry Hindley. The carved oak 'quarter jacks' are early 16th century.

CHAPTER FOUR

THE CHAPTER HOUSE

The governing body of a cathedral is known as the Chapter, so that even a secular cathedral needs a chapter house in which it can meet. Built as an office and administrative centre, it is the one part of the building which remains unconsecrated. York is lucky that its Gothic chapter house has survived, for after the Civil War in the 17th century, Oliver Cromwell abolished cathedrals and their chapters. It seemed unnecessary, therefore, to maintain their meeting place and York City Council granted one of its citizens the right to demolish it, to build stables with the stone! Luckily, the man died a week before demolition was due to commence.

Today the Chapter of York consists of the Dean, Precentor, Chancellor and Treasurer and 27 other priests from the diocese, all but the Dean, who is a Crown appointment, being chosen by the Archbishop. Although a cathedral is the bishop's church, the bishop – or in the case of York, the Archbishop – is not a member of its governing body or Chapter. Medieval archbishops sometimes did attend chapter meetings, but only by the invitation of the Dean.

The role of the Dean was meant to be that of first among equals, having presidency of the Chapter and oversight of the other cathedral clergy as his major tasks, but most medieval deans exceeded these powers. 'They say that in the church he is superior to everyone except the archbishop; and in the chapter he is superior to all.' This extract from the cathedral statutes confirms the absolute primacy of the Dean in practice. He played a dominant role in all major ceremonies of the liturgical year, taking the central position in all the associated processions. It was for him to bless the candles at the Feast of the Purification, the ashes on Ash Wednesday and the palms on Palm Sunday. More importantly, it was he who installed a new archbishop on the archiepiscopal throne. At a time when laws governed the clothes that one could wear and the accoutrements which one might carry, the sight of the Dean

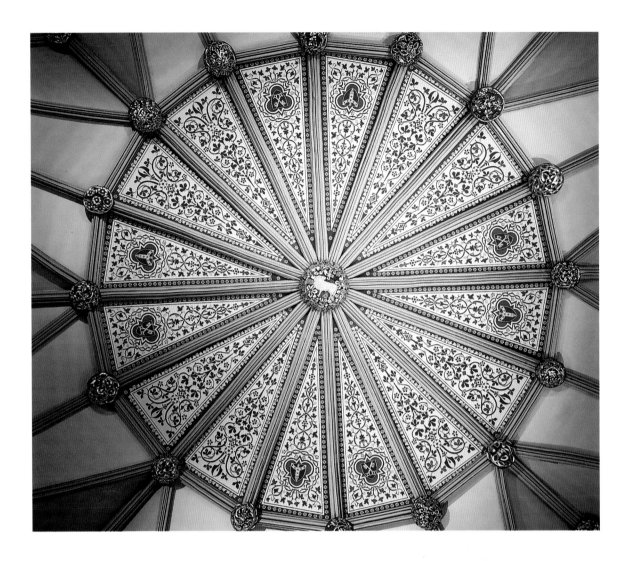

Above. The painted vaulting
of the chapter house,
restored by John Carr in
1798 and repainted in 1976.

on ceremonial progress through the city would have left no doubt as to his importance in the minds of York citizens, for he could be accompanied by 19 horses, any other canon being restricted to 5, and an entourage of 80. The 20th century is about to recognize this power officially, for the proposed Cathedrals Measure will give Deans that power they have long exercized in practice, for example giving them the casting vote at Chapter meetings.

Second in precedence to the Dean was the Precentor, whose task it was to oversee the liturgy of the cathedral and, consequently, the choir and the song school which trained the choristers. His income was poor, compared with that of the Dean, and his status also dwindled during the Middle Ages. He lost his right to precedence in the cathedral to the senior residentiary canon and most of his duties were devolved to his two deputies. Today, he is responsible for overseeing worship in the Minster.

The Chancellor has always been the third canon residentiary and his duties, as now, related to the educational work of the cathedral, including oversight of the Minster's library. Originally he also kept the Chapter's seal, but what amounted to secretarial duties were always poorly done and, from the 13th century, York has employed a lay Chapter Clerk to oversee these. There is evidence to show the existence of a grammar school run by the cathedral throughout the Middle Ages, and it is likely that it was one of the largest and most important in the country. The education of young men in theology dwindled as the universities of Oxford and Cambridge took this task to themselves, but the tradition of the cathedral hosting lectures in theology continues to this day and the names of York's Chancellors reflect the importance placed on scholarship by the cathedral.

No position in the church in medieval York was more eagerly sought after than that of Canon Treasurer of the Minster for, apart from the Dean, he was the richest of the Minster's clergy. Most of his duties were delegated to a large department of administrators. Amongst these were the equivalent of today's vergers, who were responsible for good order in the cathedral. Their failure to achieve this brought

Below and opposite below. Some of the carved heads that decorate the canopies of the stalls.

The entrance to the chapter house, showing the magnificent 13th-century ironwork on the oak door.

Opposite. View of the chapter house from Dean's Park.

constant criticism, when the peace of the building was disrupted by groups of unruly boys, or the presence of dogs, pigeons and other animals.

In the Middle Ages, the number of clergy comprising the Chapter was 36, not as many as at some of the other eight secular cathedrals, Lincoln and Wells having over 50 each, for example. The clergy at York were, however, much the best paid, their average annual income in 1291 being £48, which was £8 more than their equivalents at Lincoln. This explains why seats on York's Chapter were often given to relatives of archbishops, Popes and kings, who took the money but failed to come to the city.

The chapter house was begun in c. 1260 by masons who had worked on the north transept. It was complete and in use by 1286 when Archbishop John le Romeyn announced his intention of holding a visitation in it. Octagonal in shape, it is slightly more than 19 metres wide and 20 metres high, making it the largest in England, and it is now unique in not having a central pillar to support the timber roof, despite its immense size. It continues to be used for Chapter meetings to this day. Six canons can be seated in each of its bays, underlining the fact that no-one can take a central position and thus assume authority over the rest. The acoustics are such that it is easier to hear debate around the outer wall than when seated centrally.

The name of the master mason is unknown, but he was probably an Englishman familiar with both contemporary English court style and French Gothic architecture. The stalls are supported by mass-produced Purbeck marble shafts, which had become popular in the Early English period. There are 284 capitals and pendants, some carved in conventional stiff-leaf foliage design, others in more naturalistic form,

portraying hawthorn, oak, buttercup, strawberry and hop, for example. Remnants of paint which have survived indicate that these would have been painted originally in red or blue and enhanced with gold leaf. There is also a fine series of 237 heads, animals such as a monkey, a cat and a mouse, as well as fantastic monsters on the outer faces of the canopies.

The stained glass windows, with one exception, date from 1300–10 and demonstrate a new approach to lighting the church building. Instead of the rich, dark colours in the windows of Roger's choir, or the bright grisaille in the transepts, the glaziers have combined the two to give bands of colour across the lights, while allowing plenty of light to enter through the grisaille sections. They have introduced narrative sequences, such as scenes from the life of Christ and those of St Thomas Becket, St William of York and St Catherine. Since 1945 the York Glaziers' Trust has restored all the glass in the chapter house. The blind tracery above the entrance was never glazed, but is known to have been painted with figures. The lower niches would have held silver statues of Christ and the twelve Apostles, but these disappeared at the Reformation.

In 1798 the oak vault was replaced. Three painted panels from this original roof, a complete one depicting Synagogue and two top halves showing an archbishop and St Edmund have been preserved, but today the bosses and ribs are oak, and the infill is lath and plaster. The present ceiling design was originally painted in 1844–45 by Thomas Willement and the central panel again repainted in 1975–76 as a copy of the original. The years 1844–45 had seen a major restoration of the whole, thanks to a legacy from Dr Stephen Beckwith. This included the laying of a new floor of Minton encaustic tiles and the provision of underfloor heating. By that date about one-fifth of the original medieval carvings had been damaged or were missing, and these too were replaced.

The chapter house is linked to the Minster by a vestibule. Completed later than the two parts it was joining, it shows the difficulty the workmen had with this task, the bays, for example being of varying size and the buttresses to the north-west being misplaced. This too is unconsecrated ground and several green men, figures associated with pagan fertility rites rather than Christianity, can be found amongst the carvings. Early in the 14th century a well lit room with fireplace and garderobe was added above the vestibule. It was the drawing office for the Minster's masons and still displays evidence of their work on its gypsum floor.

The Dean and Chapter, the governing body of the Minster, sitting in their stalls.

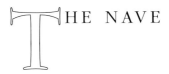HE NAVE

On 6 April 1291 Archbishop Romeyn laid the foundation stone of the new nave. The only part of Archbishop Thomas's building to have remained intact would now take 70 years to rebuild. This was not only because of the immense size of the undertaking, but also caused by other problems, such as the outbreak of the Black Death.

Adding aisles doubled the width of the earlier building, giving the Minster the widest nave in England. This posed technical problems, for the projected weight of a stone vault was feared to be too great for the walls to bear. It was decided, therefore, to roof the cathedral in wood. By the second half of the 14th century huge oaks were not plentiful, so delays were experienced whilst suitable timber was found. An ageing workforce also gave problems. In 1345 there were complaints of deep pools of water in the nave, 'such a quantity of water that lately a lad had almost been drowned'. At an inquiry, it was discovered that the master carpenter had lost his head for heights, a distinct handicap when building a vault 30 metres off the ground! He was not replaced until August 1346 – yet another delay.

It was at least 15 years before the original roof was substantially complete. Nearly five hundred years later, the nave was once again open to the elements when the vaulting was destroyed by fire. On 20 May 1840, William Groves, a watchmaker from Leeds, who had been called in to carry out repairs, left a candle burning in the south-west tower. It was not until a quarter to nine that night that passers-by became aware of the blaze it had started. Fire engines were sent by the insurance companies, the military and Lord Wenlock of Escrick Park, and the Lord Mayor sent an express train to Leeds to fetch help, but all to no avail. The watching crowd heard the ten bells crash one by one to the floor below as the fire consumed the dry timbers. Just as the crowd thought that the drama had been played out, smoke began to rise from the

Opposite. The nave looking east, empty of chairs – a reminder that this part of the Minster was not originally built for worship.

The great west window, known popularly as the 'Heart of Yorkshire' window, because of its tracery.

nave roof. Now there was a real fear that the entire building would be lost, but the bulk of the central tower eventually halted the fire's progress.

The original medieval roof was lost, but luckily detailed drawings had been made, and it was decided to use these as the basis for creating an exact copy. The key bosses of the nave roof, originally carved by Philip of Lincoln, were again created to show events from the life of Christ and his mother. There was one deliberate minor alteration, on the Nativity boss – the sight of Mary breast-feeding her son was considered too risqué for Victorian tastes, so she has, instead, been given a baby's feeding bottle.

The master masons who worked on the original nave were of high repute and consequently often wealthy men. Master Simon of York, for example, paid £1 6s 8d in tax in 1301, when two other masons paid only 1s 4d and 11d respectively. He became a freeman of the city in 1315, lived in the precincts of the Minster and requested in his will that he might be buried in the new nave. A secondary source of income for him was the carving of marble tombs, a trade common amongst master masons of the time. Another notable mason to have worked on the cathedral was Ivo de Raughton. Originally from Cumbria, he too became a freeman of the city of York, in 1317, and subsequently one of its wealthier citizens. He was a master of the English Curvilinear Decorated style, which he used not only on the west front of the Minster but also at Carlisle cathedral, Beverley and Selby.

The man responsible for paying for much of his work was arguably

The dragon's head, a pivot projecting over the nave, which may have been used to raise the font cover.

Below and opposite.
Examples of carving to be
found in the nave.

Archbishop Melton (1317–1340), a franklin's son from the East Riding, who rose to power through service in the royal household. Some see him as a great benefactor of the Minster, paying for the great west window, for example, but others question how much of his considerable fortune was lavished on the building, for he also used it to promote his family. By the time of his death, the Meltons had become one of the most richly propertied families in Yorkshire.

Melton had other calls on his income, for soon after his arrival in the city the Scots made one of their frequent incursions into England and Edward II ordered him to organize an army to stave them off. He mustered three thousand men, but they were cut to pieces by the more experienced invaders a few miles from the city at Myton-on-Swale.

Nevertheless, he left the Minster one of its finest windows – that above the western entrance, known popularly as the 'Heart of Yorkshire', because of the shape of its stone tracery. The original intention of a wall peopled by figures in glass and stone can only be imagined, for once the Reformation came to England, statues of saints were destroyed, so that the ledges on either side of the window are now empty. The figures in the glass have, however, survived, and illustrate the authority and purpose of the ministry of the church. Six hundred years of weathering eventually damaged the stonework of this window beyond repair. By 1989–90 major restoration was necessary and the entire window was re-carved. There was an exacting need for accuracy, as the original glass would later be

replaced within the new stone frame. The original stonework has been preserved for posterity, buried in Dean's Park.

The city of York is fortunate in having within its walls over half the medieval glass to have survived in England. Much of this is in the Minster and the nave glass is a prime example, for the clerestory contains panels that originally beautified Roger's 12th-century choir. The much larger lower windows date from the 14th century, when grisaille glass alone, such as that contained in the Five Sisters Window, was no longer fashionable. As in the chapter house, grisaille glass is used together with painted and stained glass to create large coloured pictures, while still allowing light into the interior.

It is clear that medieval craftsmen were aware of developments in their trades elsewhere in Europe, and the York glaziers were no exception. Silver stain, an Arab discovery, introduced to Europe through Spain, improved the look of their windows. By applying chloride of silver to white glass before firing, the glass so treated became yellow. This technique considerably reduced the number of leads needed in a window and so enhanced the quality of the pictures. It is probable that some of the nave glass illustrates the first use of this technique in England. Although the nave interior was finished around 1360, it was to be over a hundred years before the west front was complete. The twin towers were the last parts to be finished, in 1474, two years after the cathedral had been officially re-consecrated.

CHAPTER SIX

COMPLETION

The Zouche Chapel, begun by 1350, was laid out in such a way as to anticipate the subsequent rebuilding of the whole eastern arm of the cathedral, so we can safely surmise that the latter project had been envisaged before this date. There are also records showing that when Canon Thomas Sampson died in 1349, he bequeathed £20 towards the rebuilding of the choir, provided that the work was begun within a year of his death. This was too substantial a contribution to spurn. It was, nevertheless, not until 29 July 1361 that Archbishop Thoresby, who contributed two hundred pounds a year towards the rebuilding of the Minster from 1360 to his death in 1373, laid the foundation stone of this part of the cathedral.

Not only had the builders to contend with the problems of building around the existing east end, which was used for the daily office throughout the major part of the rebuilding programme, but they also had to accommodate the little church of St Mary ad Valvas which was not demolished for at least another four years. It is perhaps no wonder that roof lines do not always meet smoothly.

As often happened during the rebuilding of particular sections of the cathedral, the master mason changed and, when he did so, so did the style of the building. William Hoton the Younger succeeded his father as master mason in 1351 and was a competent but uninspired craftsman. His successor, Robert de Patryngton from the East Riding, was a man of a very different calibre, however, and the main arcades and clerestory reflect his imaginative skill.

Money problems continued to affect the speed of the work, for Archbishop Thoresby's immediate successors did not give as generously as he had done. There were also complaints during the Archbishop's visitation in 1390 that such money as had been raised had been diverted to other uses, causing yet more delay. In 1395, King Richard II supported the project with a gift of one hundred marks, following this a

Opposite. Looking down on the choir from the east window.

year later with the donation of a silver and gilt reliquary containing the bones of one of the Holy Innocents. His generosity was rewarded by the carving of his badge, a white hart, crowned and chained, on the capital of the south-east crossing pier. Another royal benefactor was the future Henry IV, as Duke of Lancaster, who exempted the Minster from paying tolls for carrying stone on the River Aire. One of the crowned heads carved on the same pier may well be a portrait of him.

This was also a time of politicking in the diocese. Not only in their care of the fabric was there a contrast between Archbishop Thoresby and his successors. John Thoresby was by nature a peace-maker, finally settling the dispute between Canterbury and York as to the primacy in England. Each Archbishop would, henceforth, be able to carry his cross in the other's province, the Archbishops of Canterbury being known as Primates of All England whilst those in York were entitled Primates of England. This settlement, Thoresby claimed, recognized the equal rank of both. Unfortunately for York, others did not interpret it in this way.

Alexander Neville, from the well known family of kingmakers, was, by contrast, universally unpopular, being described as 'a thef, a traytour, bothe to godde and to his Kyng'. He died in exile in Louvain in 1392, having been banished in 1388 for his support of Richard's favourites. During his tenure of the see, building work at the Minster ground to a halt. His successor, Thomas Arundel, ensured that this began again, exploiting his friendship with King Richard to obtain gifts to fund the work. He also achieved

Opposite. The early 18th-century wrought-iron gates were the gift of Mrs Mary Wandesford.

The pulpitum which divides the choir from the rest of the Minster is decorated with statues of the Kings of England from William the Conqueror to Henry VI.

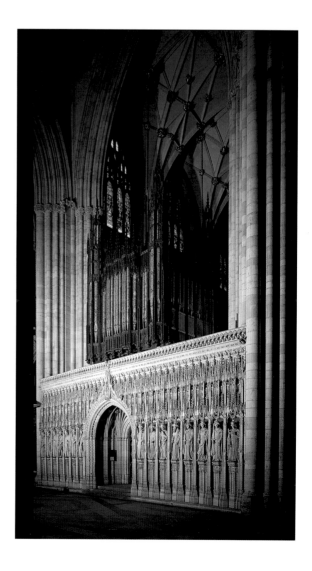

preferment for himself, being translated to Canterbury in 1396, thus demonstrating that the southern see had, in reality, won the battle for supremacy between the English provinces.

During this period, an Archbishop of York was also executed for alleged treason. Richard Scrope, a member of one of the North's most noble families, was, at the time of his enthronement, a friend of King Richard. Only a year later, however, he was not only present at the king's abdication but also read his resignation statement to Parliament. Although he had apparently become a loyal supporter of Henry IV, he was, in 1405, persuaded to take an active role in Henry Percy's

Above. John Bolton praying to Richard Scrope. An illustration from the Bolton Book of Hours.

rebellion against the king. Tricked into surrender, the Archbishop was tried at Bishopthorpe and found guilty of treason. When Scrope was brought to York for execution on the feast day of St William, the scene was being set for a martyrdom. Naively, Henry IV also allowed the executed Archbishop to be buried in the Minster, although no effigy was permitted on his tomb. It was not long before miracles were reported at his grave. Locally at least, it was accepted that 'St Richard' was responsible for these, a tradition which continued for over a hundred years. The story of Richard Scrope and Henry IV did not fully mirror that of Thomas

Details of kings from the pulpitum. From the left they are Edward III, Richard II, Stephen and Henry II. The artist has depicted Henry holding a heart. Could this be a reference to the 'Fair Rosamund'?

Becket and Henry II, however, for Richard was never canonized nor Henry IV excommunicated.

A new Archbishop needed to be elected, raising the hopes of Walter Skirlaw, Bishop of Durham. Even after the king had refused the Chapter's choice of Skirlaw for Archbishop in 1398, he had continued to be generous in his patronage of the Minster. But it was to be two and a half years before York again had an Archbishop and by then Walter was dead. He did not even live long enough to see the completion of his most generous gift, the glass to fill the great east window.

Now the largest single expanse of medieval glass to have survived anywhere in England, the tracery contains images of 109 angels, saints, martyrs, minor prophets, early Church Fathers, Saxon heroes and founders of Christianity in the North. At its apex is God the Father holding a book on which is written 'Ego sum alpha et omega' (I am alpha and omega), these being the first and last letters of the Greek alphabet. The words can be interpreted as meaning 'I am the beginning and the end'. This is the theme depicted in the rest of the glass: the top third of the panels illustrate the beginnings of the world as described in the Books of Genesis to Samuel, and the other two-thirds, the end of the world as described in the Book of Revelation. The bottom row of panels contains legendary and historical figures from York's past and includes, in the centre, Bishop Skirlaw.

Unusually, John Thornton was awarded this contract over the head of the Minster's principal glazier, John Burgh, who was employed otherwise to work on the glass of the cathedral from 1399 to 1419. Thornton's original contract has not survived, but there is a copy made by James Torre, a late 17th-century antiquarian. It stipulates that the work must be finished in three years and that he must 'portraiture the said window with historical images and other painted work in the best manner and form that he possibly could'. His efforts were to be rewarded at the rate of 4s a week, with an annual bonus of 100s if he completed the project within three years. He remained in York after the completion of the window in 1408, being made a freeman of the city in 1410. There is record of a further payment to him

The Assumption boss. This escaped damage at the time of the Reformation and can still be seen above the entrance to the choir.

Opposite. The great east window, as seen from the pulpitum.

Carvings from the altar screen, which can be seen from the Lady Chapel.

in 1433 for more work in the choir area, but this does not link his name with any particular window.

In 1407 the builders experienced another setback, when part of the central tower collapsed. In time this would have had to be rebuilt to blend with the proportions of the new cathedral, but now the work was urgent. Two reasons were given for the collapse, the first, in a letter to the Pope being 'a horrible tempest', the second, in a letter to Henry IV, 'the carelessness of the masons'. The true reason was probably neither of these, but that the tower had been significantly weakened by stresses placed on it during the constant rebuilding.

Henry IV saw his opportunity to re-establish his reputation with the Minster authorities and sent William Colchester, the master mason from Westminster Abbey, to supervise the repair work. His arrival was not greeted with delight by the York masons and a year later he and his assistant returned to London, having suffered injury at their hands. Despite this setback, William returned five years later to design and supervise the building of the present tower. This is estimated to contain 16,000 tons of masonry and much strengthening of the existing fabric was needed to bear the weight. Two screen arches were inserted at the entrances to the choir aisles, including sliding joints against the piers, to allow them to move as they adjusted to the increasing load. Colchester may also have been responsible for the inclusion of the pulpitum, which, by its strength and size, helps the eastern piers to support their share of the weight. He did not live to see the screen decorated as it is today, for the statues of the monarchs of England from William the Conqueror to Henry VI were not finished until about 1461.

There was, however, a major structural weakness, which, despite all the strengthening measures, still caused the tower to show signs of collapse. Whilst three of the crossing piers

Looking up into the central tower.

The tomb of Prince William of Hatfield (died 1346). His parents, Edward III and Philippa of Hainault, had been married in the Minster in 1328. This is the only royal burial in the cathedral, although the exact location of the grave is uncertain.

are built on firm dry ground, the fourth is built into soft, wet land. This caused uneven settlement and cracks began to appear in the masonry. Yet more strengthening was put into the foundations, but, although the movement of the tower was halted, it was recognized that to double its height, as envisaged in the original design, would also significantly increase, if not double, its weight. No-one was prepared to risk that! York Minster, consequently remains unfinished, its centre tower not significantly taller than those at the western end.

Setbacks for the builders were not yet over. Records show that in 1464 another fire broke out in the cathedral. The exact extent of the damage is not recorded, but the fire itself is mentioned in several records of the period, indicating that it was noteworthy, at a time when fires were a relatively common phenomenon in cities. It was also remembered and commented upon long after the event itself. During an archiepiscopal visitation in 1519, for example, it was recorded that the well in the crypt 'dyde grete goode what tyme as the churche was borned'.

Eventually, in 1472, the Minster was thought sufficiently near completion to warrant consecration. In reality there was still much work to be done. The western towers remained to be completed, as did battlements on several parts of the building, but on 3 July 1472 a great service of consecration was held. The largest Gothic cathedral north of the Alps was officially finished.

The east end of the Minster, showing St Stephen's chapel and the Lady Chapel bathed in sunlight.

CHAPTER SEVEN

EFORMATION AND CIVIL WAR

For just over 60 years, life in the Minster continued without major changes. Some minor alterations were made to the fabric, such as the replacement of the glass in the rose window, but the liturgy and administration continued as they had done throughout the Middle Ages. Such stability was not to continue for long, however, for the effects of the Protestant Reformation, already bringing changes on the Continent, would also be felt in England.

The early years of the 16th century were not high points in the history of the Church in general or the Minster in particular. A report made for the Dean in 1519 by the Vicars Choral and Chantry Priests, describes the cathedral as being in need of a good spring clean. Dust and cobwebs hung from walls and pillars, altar coverings were ragged and torn, and the hangings of the choir lay neglected in the vestry, covered in dog dirt and candle wax. The niceties of liturgical observance were being ignored. Vestments and altar frontals were not being changed according to season, and those which were in use, were often in need of repair. The singing of the Vicars Choral was out of tune because their music was not in good order, and candles, such as those in front of the Virgin's statue, were left unlit.

When, in 1534, Henry VIII initiated the break with Rome by declaring himself Supreme Head on Earth of the Church in England, the situation was not very much different. Archbishop Edward Lee, in his visitation report of the same year, was critical of the non-residence of the cathedral canons, and their non-attendance at services, even when they were in York. There was some substance to Thomas Cromwell's allegations that cathedral clergy 'spent their time in much idleness, and their substance in belly cheer'. Not that all archbishops were zealous in the observance of their duties either. Cardinal Wolsey, perhaps York's most famous primate, never visited the city, and Archbishop Thomas Savage (1501–1507) sent a deputy to the cathedral to be enthroned in his place. Reformation was clearly necessary.

Doorway to St Sepulchre's
Chapel. Note that the Virgin
and Child, as well as the
supporting angels, have had
their heads deliberately
severed, probably during
the 16th century.

In contrast to such cathedrals as Wells and Durham, where the Chapters positively encouraged change, no great reforming zeal swept through York. The papal tiara was chiselled from the coat of arms of St Peter in the central tower, but, generally, worship in the Minster continued as before. It is perhaps no surprise, therefore, that when Henry VIII turned his attack on the monasteries, the cathedral authorities rallied to support the protesters who had formed into the Pilgrimage of Grace. The Dissolution of the Monasteries brought significant changes to those cathedrals which had been based in monastic institutions, but as York had never housed monks, there was no need for any major alteration to its statutes. One section alone, that relating to preaching in the Minster, reflected the theological thinking of the Reformation. Henceforth, any canon with a prebend worth more than £8 per year had to contribute 6s 8d to a fund, administered by the Chancellor, for recruiting preachers, showing the increasing emphasis on the Word.

In 1541, Henry VIII made his only visit to the city and, to mark this occasion, one significant change was made in the Minster. Richard Layton, the Dean, who was more radical in his theology than the Archbishop, chose this occasion to destroy one of the two shrines of St William. The second shrine (and there are no records to tell us which was which) remained active until the reign of Edward VI, at which time Protestant observance was at its most active. In 1544, Robert Holgate, an active Protestant, was appointed to the see and was dismayed to see how few changes the cathedral had made to its daily round of worship. He compared the Minster's relationship to the diocese with that of a parasite feeding off its host. At a time when priests found themselves forbidden to drink, dice, play cards or hunt, they were allowed to marry. Holgate was one of the first to avail himself of this privilege and was, subsequently, the father of two children, giving Mary reason to imprison him in the Tower of London when she came to the throne. On 16 March 1554, he was deprived of the archbishopric for 'grave and enormous crimes and sins, especially marriage, after express profession of chastity'.

The liturgy of cathedrals changed with each succeeding Tudor monarch. In Edward's reign, Cranmer compiled two new service books, the first, written in 1549, was very moderate in its content. The second more overtly Protestant version, published in 1552, was used by the English Church (except in Mary's reign) until the second half of the next century. These Prayer Books reduced the daily office to three services – Matins, Communion and Evening Prayer, usually sung in English, although Latin was not banned in cathedrals. The introduction of worship in the vernacular brought repercussions for the wider Church, as the laity was no longer familiar with the words of the Pater Noster, Ave Maria and the Creeds. Archbishop Lee gave instructions as to how these were to be taught, also making clear that he expected his clergy to provide themselves with English Bibles for their personal study, in particular comparing the new translation with that of the Vulgate.

York citizens entering the Minster throughout the day would immediately have been aware of change. No longer were they

The tomb of Archbishop Thomas Savage. A chantry chapel has been reconstructed over his tomb.

assailed by the sound of several masses being offered simultaneously, as the chantry priests worked their way around the cathedral, celebrating at the 60 altars built for this specific purpose. These had been destroyed and, with them, the need for the priests who had lived communally in St William's College.

The theology of the Mass itself was, of course, one of the major points of dispute at this time, the wine being no longer reserved for the priest alone, but shared with the congregation. Belief in the transubstantiation of both elements was denied. The furniture of the Minster changed to reflect this: the High Altar was replaced by a wooden table, to emphasize that people were coming together to share a memorial meal rather than to witness a sacrifice.

Under the guise of religious change, the government saw the opportunity to enrich its own coffers by seizing valuables from cathedrals throughout the land. York lost silver and plate, as well as vestments, altar frontals and hangings, many of which were embroidered in gold and decorated with precious stones.

York is lucky that so much medieval glass survives within the city, for churches were ordered to destroy images, including those in the stained glass. Evidence of some defacement can still be seen in the Minster's windows, for the heads of figures are often not the original partners for the bodies. By destroying heads and faces, the Minster authorities were observing the letter of the law, whilst not committing themselves to the huge cost of replacing whole windows.

In 1553, a change in monarch brought yet more upheaval to the cathedral. Mary, a devout Catholic, wanted to return England to the papal fold. Little evidence survives, but her attempts do not appear to have met with serious opposition in York. Indeed the citizens seem positively to have welcomed the return to old, familiar ways. The High Altar was replaced and a collection of frontals built up, often bequeathed by the city's wealthier citizens in return for prayers for their souls. Mary's brief reign was not long enough, however, to re-establish the Catholic Church firmly and it was dismantled during the reign of her sister.

Unlike her father, Elizabeth I made no claim to be Head of the Church in England. She maintained that there was only one Head and that was Christ. She did want to invest power in the

Opposite. The tomb of Archbishop Matthew Hutton. His married status is shown by including his wife and sons on the monument.

monarch, however, so titled herself Supreme Governor. Elizabeth's commissioners reached York in 1559, demanding that the clergy should swear oaths of allegiance to the queen in this role. Archbishop Nicholas Heath had already refused to do so and his example was copied by nearly half the York Chapter. Faced with such conservative clergy, Elizabeth waited another two years before appointing Thomas Young as Archbishop, but it was not until the appointment of Matthew Hutton in 1567 that York again acquired a truly Protestant primate.

In Elizabeth's reign the Minster would have looked much as it had done when Edward VI was on the throne. The Communion Table replaced the High Altar, texts replaced pictures and statues, and vestments and frontals disappeared, but it was not long before cathedrals came under attack once more, this time from Puritans who wanted even greater changes. They described the canons as 'for the most part dumb dogs, unskilful sacrificing priests, destroying drones, or rather caterpillars of the word.' It is probably fair to describe the Minster at this time as an island of privilege within the city, little used by its citizens. Whereas at Winchester, for example, the mayor and corporation worshipped at the cathedral every week, at York they came only on special occasions, after the victory over the Turks at the Battle of Lepanto in 1571, for example, or to give thanks for the queen's escape from assassination in 1586.

The apathetic acceptance of cathedral by city and of city by cathedral seems to have continued until the reign of Charles I. In 1627, however, a clash over jurisdiction within the Liberty of St Peter, brought the two into open confrontation, which continued throughout the rest of the reign. The king, by contrast, took great interest in the Minster and visited the cathedral when he came to the city in 1633. He made several suggestions for improvements to the look of the building, including the demolition of the houses built against its walls.

The inability to find a uniformly acceptable common style for worship was to be one of the underlying causes of the English Civil War. As York declared for the King, but much of Yorkshire was ardently Parliamentarian, it was inevitable that the city would become involved in the conflict. In 1644 it was

Opposite. Sir William Gee and his two wives, the first of whom (on the right) was a daughter of Matthew Hutton.

under siege. As the Minster's tower, the highest point in the city, was used for signal fires to communicate with the besieged garrison at Pontefract, the cathedral became a target for enemy fire. There are records of canon balls crashing through the windows during service, then ricocheting from pillar to pillar down the nave, miraculously without causing injury to worshippers. When the city surrendered, it was agreed, in the terms negotiated with General Fairfax, that no further damage would be inflicted on the cathedral. Consequently, the Minster's glass remained safe from harm.

During the Commonwealth period, the city's ascendancy over the Minster was complete. No longer a cathedral but rather a preaching house, the archbishopric abolished and its Chapter disbanded, the civic corporation was given control, a duty which it took seriously. There was no repetition of the official looting which had taken place during the reign of Edward VI. When, for example, the great brass lectern was sold, the money raised was spent on repairs to the fabric.

The style of worship underwent further change as the Directory for Public Worship replaced the Book of Common Prayer. Extempore prayer replaced much of the set liturgy and the sermon became the focal point of the service. As accompanied singing was no longer thought desirable, the organ was dismantled.

In 1660 the Restoration saw the return of much more than the King. For the Minster, it meant the return of the Chapter and the restoration of services as before, including the use of vestments and furnishings. A new version of the Prayer Book was published in 1662; not so overtly Protestant as Cranmer's original, it better reflected the more moderate position of the Anglican Church as it had developed during the intervening years.

Relations with the city would never be as before, however, for Nonconformity had reached York. Despite the Act of Uniformity, a group of aldermen's widows protected Nonconformist worshippers, and their meeting flourished. In 1689, the Toleration Act allowed them to worship openly and in 1693 the St Saviourgate Chapel opened for worship. No longer was York a city which worshipped solely according to the rites of the Church of England.

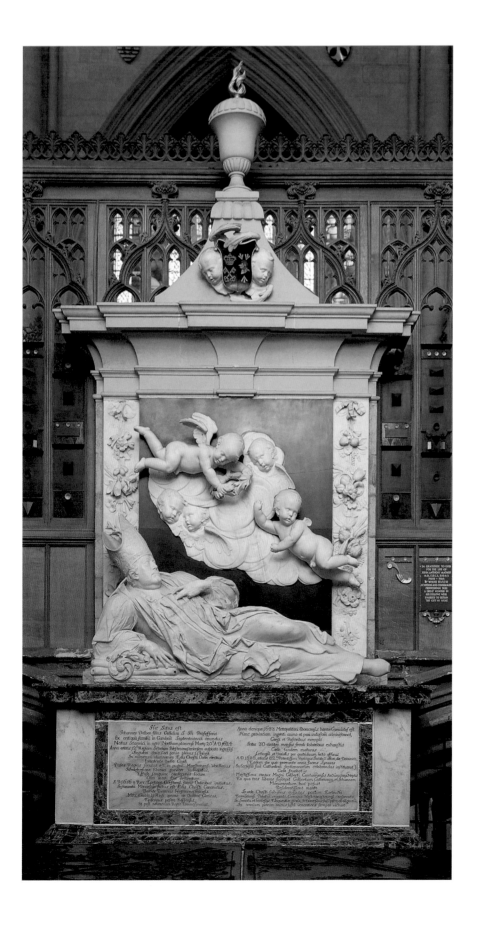

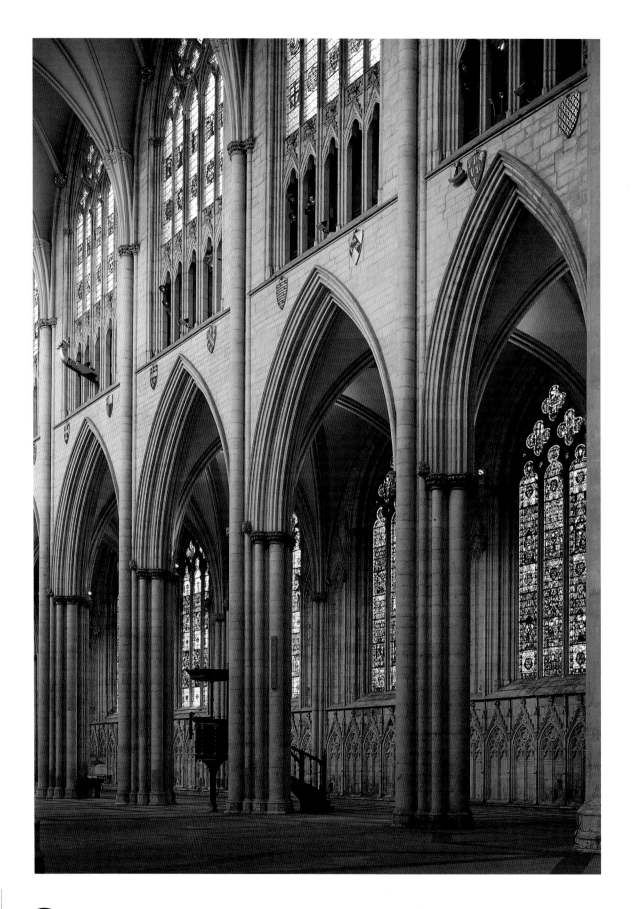

CHAPTER EIGHT

THE 18TH AND 19TH CENTURIES

The greatest change to take place in the Minster during the 18th century was the re-flooring of the nave, which began in 1731 and took seven years to complete. It was expensive. The antiquary Francis Drake claims that it cost £2,500, despite Sir Edward Gascoigne's gift of stone from his quarry at Huddleston and the re-use of marble grave slabs. Lord Burlington and his associate William Kent have been credited with the design, which is based on the Greek key pattern and reflects the revived interest in the classics prevalent at the time.

In order to realize the design every tomb that remained in the nave was destroyed, as well as many in the transepts and choir. As a result, the Minster's floor would be raised by one foot. The laying of the floor was the last real change to be made voluntarily to the building; later alterations have been in response to disaster.

Worship remained largely the same. At 6 am in summer and 7 am in winter, early prayers were said by one of the Vicars Choral, vested in gown and surplice. Daily Matins were sung at 9 am and Evensong at 5 pm. The Minster closed following this service at 6 pm. When, in 1730, Dean Osbaldeston tried to introduce a said Nicene Creed into the Communion Service, he failed because of the resistance of the residentiary canons. York remained, as ever, conservative in attitude.

The Minster also remained a bastion of the rich. Dean Osbaldeston had doors fixed to the entrances to the stalls to keep out the 'mob' or 'rabble' and restrict their use to 'the dignitaries, gentlemen and better sorts of citizens who attend divine service'. It is, therefore, not surprising that the average weekday congregation was not more than a handful in number. Laurence Sterne recorded that on All Saints' Day 1750, he preached to 'one bellows blower, three singing men, one vicar and one residentiary'.

Opposite. The nave

Not everyone remained unmoved by the experience of worshipping in the Minster, however. William Richardson, who was later to become the Precentor's assistant, recorded, 'In my return through York I strayed to the Minster. The evening service was then performed by candlelight. I had never been before in the Minster but in the midst of a summer's day. The gloom of the evening, the rows of candles fixed upon the pillars in the Nave and Transept, the lighting of the Chancel, the two distant candles, glimmering like stars at a distance on the Altar, the sound of the Organ, in the chaunts, services and anthem, had an amazing effect upon my spirits as I walked to and fro in the Nave ... I was greatly affected.'

Whilst the numbers attending service may not have been large, many citizens enjoyed coming to the Minster simply to stroll through the nave. In 1727, the Earl of Oxford described the scene: 'In the main aisle of the inside betwixt the western gate and the choir the gentlemen and ladies walk after evening service in the summer time for want of the convenience of a park and gardens, and it seems some people take as much delight in sitting here and a liberal gentleman has for that purpose covered some of the stone seats on the north side with wood above which is a brass plate with his effigies and an inscription underneath signifying his kind contribution to the health of such as were inclined to rest themselves on that bench.'

Another sign of the affection and ownership felt by the people of York for their cathedral was their response to the fire of 1753. A careless workman, whilst repairing the leading of the roof, left his chafing-dish, filled with burning coals in one of the gutters. The heat that this emitted caused the wood below the lead to begin to smoulder and, at 8 o'clock in the evening actually to burst into flame. Citizens came from all directions to fight the fire and prevented the damage from spreading to the whole building. The next year the Dean and Chapter invested in their own fire engine and buckets.

In 1757, William Peckitt, a York glass-painter, began restoration work on the great west window, renewing the heads of the Archbishops. He worked throughout the Minster for most of the second half of the century, creating new panels, such as those in the wall of the south transept, and restoring older glass. His new work, best illustrated by the figures of Abraham and Solomon, is executed in enamel paint, which was coloured by mixing powdered glass with a flux and applying it to the surface of white glass. Although his colours stand out garishly against those used by medieval glass painters, it must be remembered that he was using the best then available in Europe.

At the beginning of the next century, Dean Markham turned his attention to the outside of the building, realizing that much restoration was needed there also. The west front of the cathedral stands on the 'windiest corner in York'

The view across Dean's Park towards the Library, showing the Norman arcading.

and, consequently, the stone suffers badly from weathering. Statues that could no longer be recognized were replaced. However, Dean Markham's greatest contribution to the Minster was the re-siting of the Library, because in doing so he gave it the space to grow. He chose the derelict chapel of the medieval Archbishops' palace, and had it repaired at his own expense. He then began a policy, which continues to this day, of allowing books to be purchased as well as gifted to the collection. By the beginning of the 19th century, the stock stood at 6,000 volumes. Today it is the largest cathedral library in the country, and houses one of England's most important collections.

One of the longest-serving, but least efficient, Deans in the history of the Minster dominated the beginning of the 19th century. William Cockburn was installed in 1823 and, despite attempts to remove him, remained in office until his death in 1858.

During this period the cathedral suffered not one but two serious fires. On the night of 1–2 February 1829, Jonathan Martin, a religious fanatic, deliberately started two fires in the choir. These destroyed the woodwork, including the roof and the organ. Jonathan was soon caught, but escaped death, then the official punishment for arson. Instead he was locked in Bedlam, the London hospital for the insane, for the remaining nine years of his life. The public responded to the disaster with great generosity and, whilst not raising the total cost of the restoration, did donate sufficient to make speedy repair possible.

One outcome of the disaster, the value of which could not have been anticipated, was the employment of John Browne to make detailed drawings of the Minster's decorations. The lack of such a record had been felt when the fire damage was repaired, but little did people realize

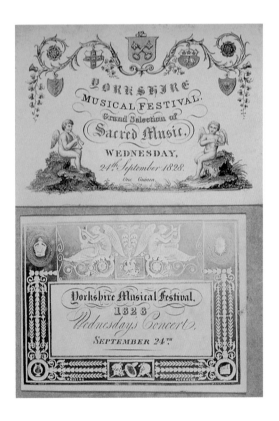

A ticket for the 1828 music festival.

Opposite. The upper hall of the Library. The Gothic style of the architecture is a reminder of the original purpose of the building.

how vital those drawings would be just 11 years later to the accurate reconstruction of the nave roof, when this in turn fell victim to fire, as mentioned previously.

This time it was carelessness that caused the blaze, for a watch repairer had left his candle burning in the south-west tower. Not surprisingly, the public was slower to respond, but the task of replacing the nave roof and restoring the gutted south nave aisle and south-west tower was enormous. By the 1850s, the Minster was deep in debt, causing general maintenance to come to a halt. In consequence, a survey of 1842 showing weaknesses in the piers of the central tower had to be ignored.

The finances of the Minster were at a low ebb. Income

The memorial for William Wentworth, 2nd Earl of Strafford and his wife in All Saints' Chapel. The Marquis of Rockingham, Prime Minister 1765-66 and 1782, is among the family buried in this vault.

from endowments had been lost through an Act of Parliament of 1840, which diverted this money to finance new industrial parishes. In his attempt to open up the land around the Minster, Dean Cockburn had also destroyed property and, with it, the income generated by rents. In an attempt to remedy this, he sold the metal of the bells

Thomas Wentworth (died 1723) and his wife.

Top. The orchestra arranged in front of the pulpitum for a music festival in the Minster.

Above. The audience sitting in specially built banks of seats for a music festival.

Opposite. The empty nave looking west. In January each year the furniture is removed so that its size and space can be appreciated.

destroyed by the 1840 fire, leaving himself open to the charge that he had sold Minster property for his own gain.

He had a well connected enemy amongst his own clergy, for Archbishop Harcourt's son was one of the residentiary canons. The Dean had not endeared himself to the Chapter. Having decided to destroy the old Deanery, as part of the clearance of the Minster precincts, he needed another site on which a new house could be built. The Chapter Clerk, a lawyer, had serious reservations about the way in which this was acquired. The Chapter itself was even more alarmed about the building, for the Dean had given imprecise instructions to the architect, who seriously overspent as a result; and it was the Chapter that had to foot the bill.

A third complaint against the Dean was, once again, probably the result of his poor administrative skills rather than deliberate fraud. After the Archbishop's Visitation of 1841, he found himself accused of simony. The practice of selling positions in the Church has always been illegal. It was, however, perfectly legitimate for some money to change hands when an appointment was made. Dean Cockburn inadvertently strayed over the fine line which separated the permissible from the forbidden, by no means difficult for such a muddled administrator! The hearing in the Consistory Court took 14 days. He was not helped by his own impetuosity, for he stormed out mid-trial and, on another occasion, was charged with contempt of

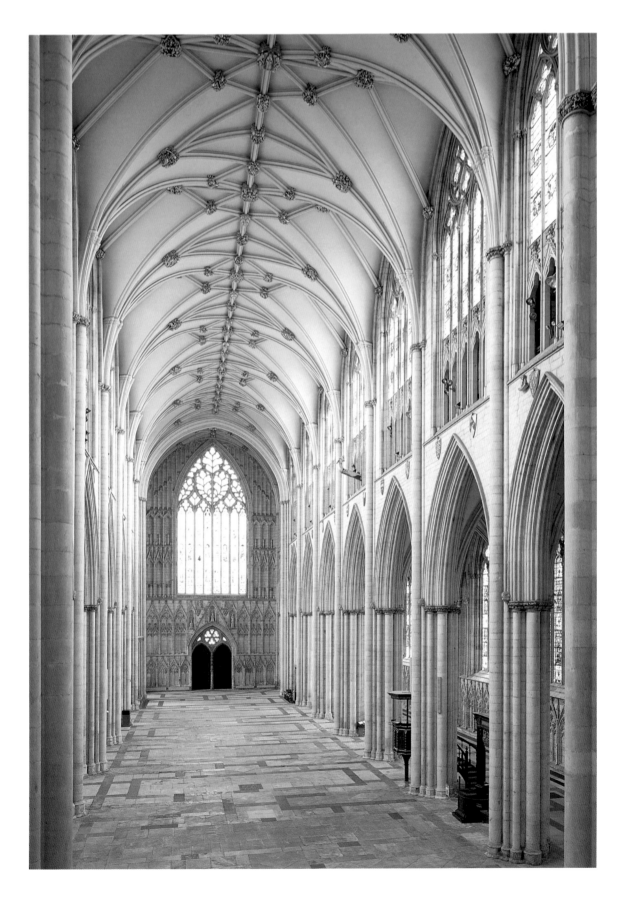

court. It is perhaps not surprising, therefore, that he was found guilty and deprived of his living. Knowing himself to be innocent, he appealed to the Queen's Bench, where the verdict was overturned, to the great joy of the people of York.

It would be unfair to dwell only on the disasters of his term of office, for Dean Cockburn was also a man of vision. Between 1823 and 1835, he supported four music festivals in the Minster, raising money for four Yorkshire hospitals, as well as putting the cathedral at the heart of York's cultural and social life. To cope with the crowds, extra seating was added in temporary galleries in the nave, and the choirs were seated in tiers in front of the pulpitum.

Liturgically, however, the Minster did suffer and, for a time, there was not even a weekly Communion, let alone a daily celebration. The education of the cathedral's choristers was also threatened. When, in 1828, St Peter's School moved to a new building on the old Deanery site, the choir boys were considered too humble to be amongst the pupils and they were moved to the Training School in Monkgate. This in turn acquired new buildings and consequently increased its fees. One guinea per quarter per pupil was considered too much by the Dean and Chapter, who immediately transferred the choristers to the Manor School. In 1850, this was housed in an upstairs room in Petergate and charged only a penny a week. The master was Mr 'Terry' Ainsworth, who was noted for having only one arm, the other being a cork replica with a large iron hook in place of a hand. His method of dealing with recalcitrant boys was to take the cane in his left hand, grab them with the hook of the right and beat them into submission! This was just one of the problems facing Dean Duncombe when he took up office in 1858.

Dean Duncombe had no obvious qualification except great wealth for this appointment, but, in the event, he provided the stability which the Minster badly needed after Dean Cockburn's government. He rescued the cathedral from the financial chaos into which it had been plunged, and re-started the programmes of restoration which had

Opposite. A page from one of the Books of Hours housed in the Minster Library.

been halted. Realizing that the new railway was bringing many tourists to the city, he also began to clear the view of the Minster from the Lendal Bridge approach, creating Duncombe Place.

For the first time in the Minster's history, an effort was made to attract working people to worship in the cathedral, by installing gas lighting and heating from coke boilers, as well as putting benches in the nave. The Dean then instituted special Sunday evening services, which were less formal in style than those of the daily office.

For all this, Dean Duncombe was a liturgical traditionalist, having been influenced by the High Church movement during his time at Oxford. Evidence of his own churchmanship can be seen in his re-introduction of the full Choral Eucharist, York being the first English cathedral to sing this since the Reformation. He also favoured a more formal look to worship and, for example, put the choir back into cassocks, surplices and ruffs instead of the fur-trimmed jackets they had been wearing. He took a step too far, however, when in 1866 he re-furnished the High Altar with a new set of frontals. Opposition was vehemently expressed in the local press, especially to the side panels of the Trinity frontal, which had been embroidered with lilies. These, the symbol of the Virgin Mary, confirmed people's worst fears – the Dean was a secret Papist! Despite this small hiccup, by the time of his death in 1880 the style of worship that he had brought to the cathedral was common in Anglican churches throughout England, and would continue unchanged for many years.

William Cockburn, Dean 1822–1858.

THE 20TH CENTURY

The 20th century has been no less eventful than those that went before. A threat of collapse to the central tower, fire in the south transept and changes in liturgy, more radical than any since 1662, have all played their part. Added to these, as the century draws to a close, there are far-reaching changes to the governance of cathedrals and their accountability, a concept unknown in previous centuries. All this has happened against a background of growing ecumenism, which has already led to agreements with some of the Protestant Churches on the continent and may lead to talks of unity with other denominations in this country. Nor have Catholic links been neglected, and York has been active in promoting these, beginning with the discussions with Cardinal Suenens of Malines, Belgium, as early as the 1920s. Surprisingly, in an age which is overtly less Christian than any of its predecessors, there has been an explosion in the number of visitors to cathedrals. It has been estimated that two and a quarter million people enter York Minster each year.

In 1967, Bernard Feilden, the newly appointed Surveyor of the Fabric, began a survey of the cathedral, a major work which took two years to complete. This revealed a structural crisis so serious that the collapse of the entire building seemed a real possibility. Both the east and west walls were out of true, leaning away from the rest of the building, and needed massive strengthening to the foundations if they were to remain standing. More serious, however, was severe cracking and movement in the masonry of one of the central tower piers below ground level. It was estimated that if drastic repairs were not carried out within 15 years, the structure would be too fragile to take the strain of repair at all. The sum of two million pounds was urgently needed to underwrite the project. Despite fears of incurring huge debts, should public generosity not match the amount required, work had to begin immediately.

A new post, that of High Steward, was created and offered by the Archbishop, on behalf of the Dean and Chapter, to Lord

A typical crack in the
stonework, showing the
urgency of the restoration
programme.

Protecting the organ whilst
work was in progress on the
central tower.

Scarborough. His role was to co-ordinate the appeal to raise the money. Such was the interest that the project engendered, because of the technical skills needed to carry it out and the opportunities for a thorough archaeological survey of the site whilst the work was going on, as well as the ultimate goal of preserving one of Europe's greatest cathedrals, that the money was raised by 1972. This coincided with the completion of the project and the five hundredth anniversary of the consecration of the building in 1472. The opportunity had also been taken to clean the interior, paint and gild the bosses and to begin cleaning the outside. It was estimated that two million visitors came to York that year and most of them spent time in the Minster, seeing it as it had not been seen for years.

Visitors can still inspect the great concrete collars and steel rods which now underpin the building, for instead of filling in the enormous space cleared amongst the foundations of the central tower in order to carry out the work, the Dean and Chapter decided to utilize it and develop it as a museum. At first called The Undercroft, now The Foundations, it became a display area for artefacts found during the excavations, as well as showing the technology used for the rescue. It was hoped that this would help visitors to understand the chronology of the site.

The test of the engineering involved came with the 1984 fire. This conflagration, caused according to the official report by lightning hitting the timbers within the south transept roof space, at one stage looked as though it might spread throughout the building. A fire-break was needed and the only way that one could be created was by pulling the remaining timbers away from the central tower. The firemen knew the tower's history. Would sixteen thousand tons of stone crash to the ground as they pulled? Given that the Minster would be destroyed if no attempt were made, the gamble seemed worth taking. So it proved, for the tower's structure withstood the forces acting upon it.

On the morning of 9 July 1984, when the Minster staff assessed the damage, they found that it was severe enough. The south transept roof had been completely destroyed and the whole building filled with corrosive soot and smoke. Once again

Shoring up the east end of the Minster, so that the foundations of the cathedral could be strengthened.

The *Blue Peter* bosses.

Below. 'Fire of York
Minster'. Ten-year-old Laura
Smith thought of the rose
window, in which you can
find Tudor roses,
surrounded by flames.

Above. 'Man on the Moon'
designed by six-year-old
Rebecca Welsh. Each boss
took a carver five or six
weeks to complete.

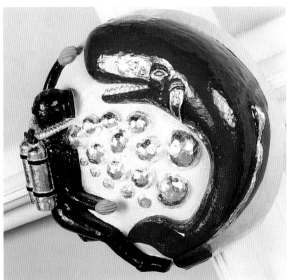

Right. Seven-year-old
Richard Gaston celebrated
attempts to 'Save the
Whales'. Once carved, a
painter finishes the boss.

Left. 'Famine Relief' by 15-year-old Tim Hutchinson, recalls the disastrous famine which hit Ethiopia. This reflects the contemporary theme, inviting young people to consider events in the world in which they lived.

Right. 'Raising the Mary Rose' by 16-year-old Joanne Biggs. Henry VIII's warship was being excavated by archaeologists at the time of the fire and restoration.

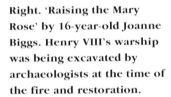

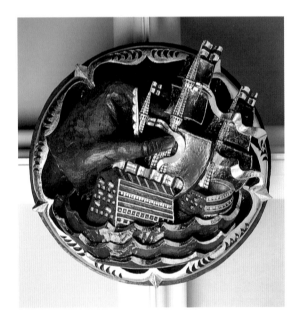

Left. 'Conquest of Space' by eight-year-old Ben Kerslake reminds us how space exploration dominated this decade of world history.

The rose window in the gable of the south transept.

the public rallied to the Minster's plight and sent money. As the restoration was paid for by the insurance companies, advantage of these donations was taken to put enhanced lighting on the newly created vault and to install a sophisticated smoke-detection system throughout the building.

The new vaulting particularly caught the public's imagination when the cathedral authorities decided to include some children's work in the design. *Blue Peter*, the children's television programme, agreed to organize a competition in which their viewers were asked to create a design for one of the new bosses. From over 32,000 entries, six were chosen as winners, and then carved and painted in the Minster's workshops.

The rose window, riddled with forty-thousand heat-cracks, also needed extensive restoration. This caught the public imagination as well, especially when, half-complete, it was set above a mirror in the chapter house, so giving the impression of the whole. People enjoyed the opportunity to see some of the Minster glass so close at hand.

The final piece of restoration work, which should be completed before the millennium, is that of the great west door. The window above it, the Heart of Yorkshire, has already been completely recarved, because the mullions and tracery were weathered beyond repair. The doorway had become equally worn and in need of the same treatment, but here there was an additional problem to be overcome. Whilst remaking the window required the skilful carving of masonry, it did not require more than the reproduction of what existed. The carvings around the door were, by contrast, so damaged that they gave few clues as to their subject matter. In 1736, Francis Drake had indicated that they showed the Adam and Eve story, but modern scholars suggested that other scenes were depicted as well. Permission

A gilder at work on one of the newly carved south transept bosses.

Cain and Abel. One of the scenes designed by Rory Young as part of a Genesis cycle which is to surround the west door.

was sought, therefore, to carve a completely new doorway, medieval in spirit but not restricted to the medieval in its interpretation. Rory Young has designed a new Genesis cycle, which is being carved in the Minster's Stoneyard and then fitted in place. Traditional skills continue to be exercized, whilst adding something of our own time to the building.

Two Minster Deans have, this century, been involved in the

development of the liturgy. Dean Milner-White introduced to the cathedral the Service of Nine Lessons and Carols, originally devised by him when he was Dean of King's College, Cambridge. This has now become a traditional part of the cathedral's year and is considered the Minster's Christmas gift to the City. For over four thousand people, Christmas begins at 4 o'clock on Christmas Eve when, sitting in the crowded Minster, they hear the treble voice of a boy chorister singing the opening verse of 'Once in Royal David's City'.

Noah. One of the newly carved voussoirs for the west door.

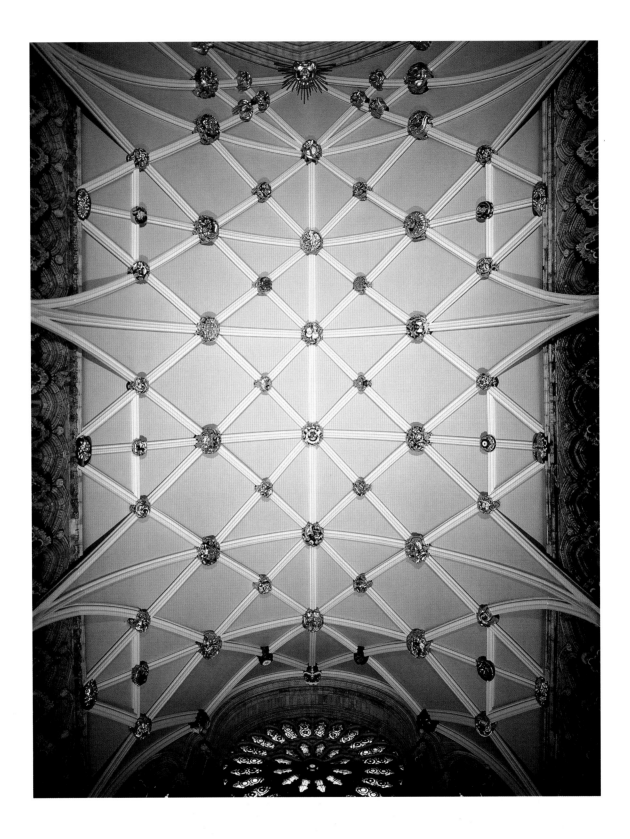

**The restored vault of the
south transept.**

More notable, because it affected the liturgy of the Church of England as a whole, was the contribution of Dean Ronald Jasper, who led the Liturgical Commission which revised the 1662 Prayer Book and developed the Alternative Service Book to take its place. Published in 1980, this attempted to devise a form of words which would allow people to worship in the language of our time. Whilst not popular with all, it did attempt to meet the criticism that the Church had no relevance for the late 20th century. He himself was under no illusion that it would last as long as its predecessor, nor was that ever his intention.

The present Dean, Raymond Furnell, has also played a part in ensuring that cathedrals, sometimes accused of being anachronisms, survive into the next century. He has been a member of the group which looked at the implementation of the findings of the Archbishop's Commission on Cathedrals. The Cathedrals Measure 1996 is introducing the most far-reaching changes for York since Thomas first established the Chapter of 1080. New bodies, called Cathedral Councils, will bring a wider field of people into the governing bodies, giving the laity an opportunity to enter what has been until now an entirely clerical preserve.

The late 20th century sees the various denominations within the Church trying to work more closely than they have ever done before. The Minster is very welcoming as a venue for ecumenical worship and recognizes that, as the largest church in York, it can host multi-denominational events, such as *One Voice*, in a way that no other venue can. As a representative of the Anglican tradition, a Church based on Elizabeth I's desire to find middle ground, it is well placed to negotiate with both the Catholic and Free Church traditions.

Its prime function now, as when it was first built, is to offer worship on a daily basis, to continue the cathedral tradition of excellence in all it does, for the glory of God.

Dean Ronald Jasper.

Burying the stonework from the original great west window.

PLAN SHOWING
NORMAN AND ROMAN LAYERS
BENEATH YORK MINSTER

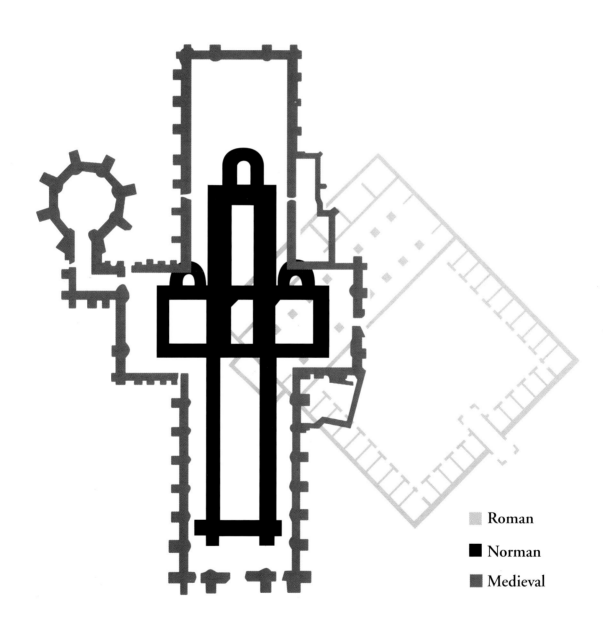

Roman

Norman

Medieval

N

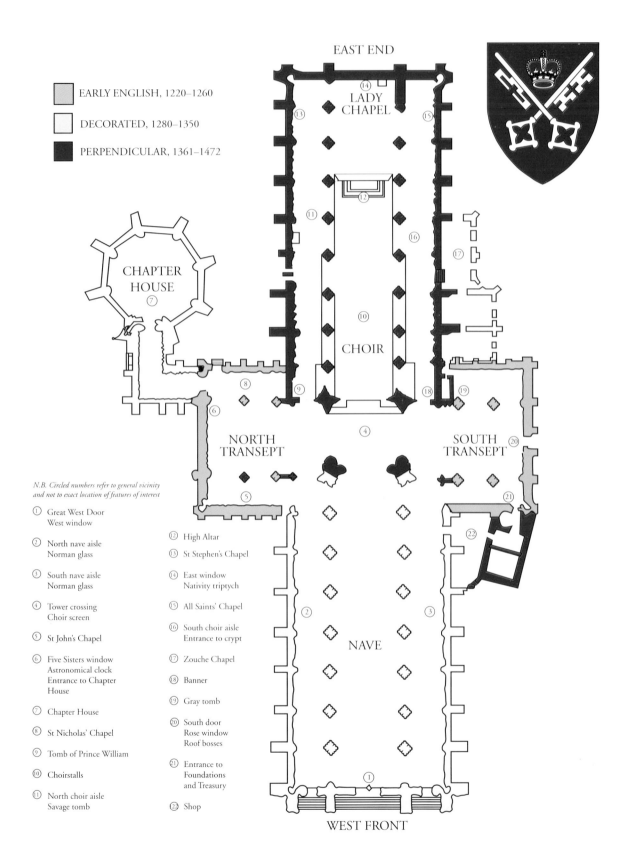

EAST END

PERPENDICULAR, 1361–1472

DECORATED, 1280–1350

EARLY ENGLISH, 1220–1260

LADY CHAPEL

⑭

⑬

⑮

⑫

⑪

⑯

⑰

CHAPTER HOUSE
⑦

CHOIR

⑩

⑧

⑨

⑱

⑲

⑥

④

NORTH TRANSEPT

SOUTH TRANSEPT

⑳

⑤

N.B. Circled numbers refer to general vicinity and not to exact location of features of interest

① Great West Door
West window

② North nave aisle
Norman glass

③ South nave aisle
Norman glass

④ Tower crossing
Choir screen

⑤ St John's Chapel

⑥ Five Sisters window
Astronomical clock
Entrance to Chapter House

⑦ Chapter House

⑧ St Nicholas' Chapel

⑨ Tomb of Prince William

⑩ Choirstalls

⑪ North choir aisle
Savage tomb

⑫ High Altar

⑬ St Stephen's Chapel

⑭ East window
Nativity triptych

⑮ All Saints' Chapel

⑯ South choir aisle
Entrance to crypt

⑰ Zouche Chapel

⑱ Banner

⑲ Gray tomb

⑳ South door
Rose window
Roof bosses

㉑ Entrance to
Foundations
and Treasury

㉒ Shop

②

③

NAVE

㉑

㉒

①

WEST FRONT

N